IMAGES
of America

GLENCOE
MILL VILLAGE

GLENCOE MILL
1880 - 82

Incorporated in 1880 by James H. and William E. Holt, sons of textile pioneer E.M. Holt. The last water-powered textile mill developed by the Holts. Produced napped cotton cloth, flannels and woven plaids. Employed as many as 500 workers at its height. Closed in 1954. Acquired by Preservation North Carolina in 1997.

Highway historical markers briefly describe the story of Glencoe, its mill, and its village. These markers stand at the two entrances to the community in Alamance County. The once-thriving mill village became a community falling into ruin. Now in the National Register of Historic Places and returning to life, Glencoe holds a special place in North Carolina's textile history. (Author's collection.)

ON THE COVER: This 1908 photograph shows students in front of the two-room school that served the Glencoe Mill village for several decades. Sixth from right in the front row is Nathan Pennington, and beside him is his twin sister, Lila. Both would work at the mill. A new school with six rooms was constructed in 1936 as a Public Works Administration project. (Courtesy of Patsy Pennington Harwood.)

IMAGES
of America

GLENCOE
MILL VILLAGE

Don Bolden

ARCADIA
PUBLISHING

Copyright © 2015 by Don Bolden
ISBN 978-1-5316-7825-8

Published by Arcadia Publishing
Charleston, South Carolina

Library of Congress Control Number: 2015936184

For all general information, please contact Arcadia Publishing:
Telephone 843-853-2070
Fax 843-853-0044
E-mail sales@arcadiapublishing.com
For customer service and orders:
Toll-Free 1-888-313-2665

Visit us on the Internet at www.arcadiapublishing.com

*To Billie Faye, who has endured many years of my obsession
with Alamance County history and smiled through it all.*

CONTENTS

ACKNOWLEDGMENTS

A number of people played key roles in the production of *Glencoe Mill Village*, but no one more so than Jerrie Nall, the driving force behind the Textile Heritage Museum now located in the village. Jerrie not only provided photographs from the museum's collection, but she sought out others from former residents and their family members. She tracked down people in other states who had Glencoe photographs from many years back.

The Reverend Jack Phillips made photographs available from his family records. He grew up as one of 11 children in a mill house in the village.

James "Dink" Holland also lived in the village, and a number of pictures in the book came from his family. Roslyn Sumner of Georgia provided Murray family photographs, and others came from the Marshall family. Thanks, too, for photographs from the files of the *Burlington Times-News*.

Greg Harwood deserves special thanks. He made a trip from his home in New Jersey to the Maryland home of his mother, Patsy Pennington Harwood, to pick up the photograph you see on our cover, along with others inside. Thanks, too, to Ann Hobgood, a village resident, who provided information and key contacts.

Contributors of photographs are credited at the end of the captions. Images from the Textile Heritage Museum are credited to THM. Unless otherwise credited, photographs are from my personal files or were made by me in the production of the book.

Special thanks to Sharon McAllister, my editor at Arcadia Publishing. When I had a question, she had the answer—quickly.

INTRODUCTION

In the early 1800s, the manufacture of textile products in the United States was centered in the New England states, with many products still imported from England.

The southern United States was the major cotton-producing area at the time, but few mills were in operation there. Growers shipped their cotton north and then bought the finished goods made in Northern mills. Northern mill owners, of course, strongly opposed textile operations in the South, but there were those Southerners who believed they could successfully compete with the Northern mills.

One of those was Edwin M. Holt, who lived on the farm of his father, Michael Holt III, in the North Carolina Piedmont. He also ran a machine shop and a general store for his father. His work brought him in contact with a Greensboro man who operated a small cotton-yarn factory. It was one of only four of its kind in the state at the time. In that little cotton mill, Holt saw opportunity. It was costing cotton farmers dearly to send their product north to be processed and then have to buy products, which had to be shipped back.

Holt enlisted his brother-in-law William Carrigan as a partner, and they established their mill in 1837 along the banks of Great Alamance Creek. It was situated in a remote place between the trade areas of Greensboro and Hillsborough.

Carrigan's wife died in 1851, and he went back to his home in Arkansas. By then, Holt's son Thomas was working in the mill. The facility had been successful since its beginning, but it was doing pretty much what other Southern mills were doing: making cotton products that were then shipped north to be dyed and processed.

In 1853, that changed. A Frenchman came to the Holt mill and offered to show the Holts how to dye cloth in exchange for payment of $100 and a place to live. That allowed the Holts to begin production of a colored fabric known today as Alamance Plaids. The knowledge of dyeing fabrics led to great success at Alamance and in several other mills begun by the Holt family in the years that followed. It made the Holts one of the most prominent textile families in North Carolina history.

E.M. Holt had several sons, and most of them learned the textile business from their father. Holt bought a mill operation at Haw River in 1858, and son Michael took over that operation. In 1869, E.M. Holt's sons J.H. Holt, W.E. Holt, and L. Banks Holt and his son-in-law J.N. Williamson opened a mill at the village of Carolina. That mill operated for almost 100 years, and its buildings still stand by the river.

Lawrence Holt and L. Banks Holt opened a mill in 1879 just downstream from the first Holt mill on Great Alamance at a site to be known as Bellemont. Son-in-law J.N. Williamson and his sons opened the Ossipee Cotton Mill in 1878. The plant was just a short distance upstream from Glencoe.

Actually, when each of those mills was constructed, a new village was born. Housing had to be provided for workers, a company store was necessary, and schools and churches sprang up nearby. Mill workers in those days lived almost entirely within the village all year long.

The river, of course, was essential to the operations of a textile mill. Until the 1880s, water was the only source of power to operate the machinery in the plants.

In the 1870s, J.H. Holt had children who were going to need places to work, and Carolina was becoming crowded. So he began to look at new locations. Just upstream from Carolina was a tobacco-processing plant with several buildings that would accommodate a textile operation. That property was owned by Moses and Levi Vincent, and in 1878, E.M. Holt and his sons James and William bought the property. A year later, James and William bought more adjoining property and began construction in 1880.

There was already a millrace there, having served a gristmill on the site, so the Holts improved it and built a dam of logs and stones across Haw River. From there, water was diverted into the mill's power plant to provide the necessary means to operate its equipment. Therein lies a distinction for Glencoe Mill. It was the last of the several mills along Haw River to use water for power.

James and William Holt operated Glencoe Mill until 1897, when Robert Holt, son of James, took over the business until 1924. At that time, another child of James Holt, Lelia Daisy Holt, assumed control. She was married to Walter Guerry Green of Charleston, South Carolina. Daisy Green's two sons, Holt Green and Walter Green Jr., followed her in the operations. Both served in the Navy during World War II, but only one, Walter, came back. Holt Green was an OSS officer for the Navy during the war. He was sent on an espionage mission behind German lines in Eastern Europe and was captured. He was executed as a spy. Walter Green Jr. headed the Glencoe operations when he came home.

During World War II, a number of young men in the village went off to war, and at least one, Marshall Hurley, was killed.

The mill grew quite well over the years, and in the 1940s, there were more than 5,000 spindles and some 200 looms in operation. As the 1950s dawned, it was obvious that things were changing for Glencoe. Smaller cotton mills were merging and gaining a bigger share of the market and increasing competition for Glencoe. Finally, in 1954, the situation proved too much for Glencoe, and the mill was closed.

The closing, however, did not end the memories of those who had been born there, worked there, went to school and church there, and shared the friendship of others who followed the same path.

Billie Phillips was one of those who grew up in the Glencoe village, and he produced a book, *Growing Up in Glencoe*, some years ago. He wrote that, by 1881, the mill had 3,120 spindles and 186 looms producing plaid, striped, and checkered cloth that was sold through agents in New York City. Phillips said that in the 1890s, Glencoe Mill operated 292 days per year, and employees worked 11 hours per day, six days a week.

In 1890, according to Phillips, the North Carolina Bureau of Labor Statistics showed 40 men, 57 women, 20 boys, and 16 girls employed at the mill. Entire families worked there, with children working alongside their parents. Pay was quite low, a few dollars a week for a skilled male worker, with less for unskilled, women, and children. By 1924, according to Phillips, wages ranged from $2.10 per week to $6.60 per week.

The mill owners constructed 41 mill houses, some with three rooms, others with five. Rent was $1.40 to $2 a month in 1894. One man who grew up in the village remembered living in five different houses. He said that, when a family moved out of one of the better houses, residents in the smaller units had the opportunity to move up to the better house, depending on the time they had lived in the village. When someone lost a job at the mill, it was only part of the loss. The individual also lost housing.

The houses, of course, had no indoor plumbing, so residents depended on the outhouse behind the residence. Wells filled the need for water. Some houses had individual wells, while other wells served more than one house. Houses were built on pillars of brick and left open underneath. Larger houses were two stories, with a staircase in the middle of the house. The main source of heat was the fireplace, and if one was sleeping upstairs, not much of that heat reached them. Some houses had cook stoves fueled by kerosene, which added to the heat.

A wooded area just east of Front Street separated the modest mill houses from a very large house, where the mill owner lived. One former resident of the community, Earl Councilman, said, "That house was an elite type of place; they had a butler and everything." There were a couple of smaller houses near it, and one of them was home to Richard Duck, the cook and butler for the owners.

The village also had a tiny barbershop, and there was a lodge hall for the Junior Order of the Union of American Mechanics, a fraternal group of which many men of the village were members. It was a place of mystery for the youngsters, some of whom were afraid to go near the building. The barbershop has been restored, but the lodge hall is in a state of disrepair.

One of the most important places in the village for the workers was the company store. It was, of course, owned and operated by the mill, and it was there that the workers bought their food and other needs. The store sold shoes, work clothes, hardware, and just about anything anyone in the village needed.

For many years—from 1916 to the 1940s—James Waddell ran the store. He began at 6:30 a.m. and remained open until 9:00 p.m. He had an assistant who helped after his mill shift was over. The store was in the building with the company office, and mill employees were paid out of the store, not the office. Thursday was payday, and money came from the bank on Wednesday. Every Wednesday night, Waddell slept in the store with his shotgun nearby.

On Thursday, the money was placed in an envelope with the worker's name on it. Each was placed in a slot in a drawer, and from there, they were given to the worker, not to a spouse or any other family member. After the worker received the pay, Waddell asked how much was to be paid on the account at the store.

Waddell also handled the mail for the village. It came to him in a big bag, and he put it into the proper slots in the store so it could be picked up.

Glencoe School was at the upper end of Front Street. (There were two streets in the village, Front Street and Back Street.) In the beginning, it was a two-room school in a frame building. In 1936, it was replaced with a modern brick structure. Although not used today, the building remains. Students went to high school at Pleasant Grove High. The school was not provided by the mill owners but was a part of the Alamance County School System.

There were two churches, a Methodist church and a Baptist church. The Methodist church was in the middle of the village, and the Baptist church was built at the north end of Front Street. The Methodist Church has moved away, but Glencoe Baptist Church remains a part of the community, as it has been since October 19, 1893.

There is one building related to the mill that is not in the village. The building sat a mile or two west of the mill, atop a high hill that overlooks Haw River. Called Fort Snug, it was a retreat for the mill owners. They used it for weekend respites and as a place to entertain guests. It burned down many years ago, but its foundation remains atop that hill and now overlooks the 11th green of Indian Valley Golf Course.

After the mill closed, some people continued to live in the village for a while, but it finally became almost deserted and was in danger of being lost. However, some years ago, Myron and Sarah Rhyne of Graham purchased a part of the property. Sarah Rhyne worked hard for restoration and preservation of the area as a National Historic Site. She traveled to Washington, DC, and successfully argued her case. The designation was given in 1979. In 1997, she gave her property to Preservation North Carolina, and it, in turn, purchased the remaining property and began the restoration.

Many homes are now restored and privately owned. Sections of the mill are occupied by various private operations, and Burlington is planning a nature museum there.

The Textile Heritage Museum is open in the store and office building, and it attracts visitors from across the nation. Exhibits and displays tell the story not only of Glencoe, but of Southern textiles in general. A number of special events are held at the museum, including antique car shows, visits by bicycling groups, and events to honor veterans. The highlight of the year is the annual Christmas tour of the village, with homes decorated for the holidays and open to visitors.

The North Carolina Mountains to the Coast Hiking Trail passes through the village, and there are many recreational activities available on and along the river. There is a canoe entry point on the river at the entrance to the village.

As the result of the efforts of many people over the past several years, Glencoe is no longer dying and decaying. The mill village has found new life and looks to a healthy future.

One

GLENCOE
THE MILL AND THE VILLAGE

The Glencoe Mill and its village lie just north of Burlington, North Carolina, on Highway 62 along the banks of the Haw River. The mill closed in 1954, but the area today is known as Glencoe Mill Village Historic District, a National Historic Site since 1979. It is unique in that the mill building and other structures to house hydroelectric production, dyeing, and other supporting operations are still intact, as are many of the original 41 mill houses built for company employees. The dam that served the mill remains. It is some 250 feet long and 8 feet high.

Glencoe is one of the few places in the nation where one can see a water-powered textile operation from the 1800s still much as it was in its days of peak production. For many years, most of the mill buildings and houses were vacant following Glencoe Mill's closing, and, with passing time, they fell into disrepair. However, thanks to the interest of certain individuals, including Sarah Rhyne of Graham, efforts began to restore the properties and preserve them for future generations. Sarah and her husband, Myron, owned part of the area in the late 1900s, and it was largely through her efforts that historic district status was obtained.

Today, the mill office and company store have been converted into the Textile Heritage Museum, and many of the old mill houses have been purchased and restored by private individuals. Other mill buildings are used for varied businesses, including an art studio. Walking through the area today, one sees houses of various bright colors along the street, along with a few that are still in disrepair, awaiting owners who will restore them. Many people across the nation visit the village and the museum each year now, taking a look at a community that is truly a page from the history of Southern textiles.

This aerial photograph shows Glencoe as it appeared in the 1940s, when the mill was operating at full capacity. The mill, built by sons of textile pioneer E.M. Holt, produced its power using the water of the Haw River, which flows away to the south, joins the Cape Fear River, and eventually flows into the Atlantic Ocean. It was one of several mills in Alamance County—and the last—to use water from the Haw River to generate power for operations. Later mills in the area used steam power and were located away from the river. Carolina Mill, another operation of E.M. Holt's heirs, is located just a mile down the river. Glencoe Mill began operations in 1880 and closed in 1954. The village declined over the years, but in the late 1900s, restoration began. Today, many of the homes have been restored and are occupied, and the company store is now home to the Textile Heritage Museum. (THM.)

This second aerial photograph of the Glencoe village was made at the same time as the previous one. Taken from the opposite side of the village, it shows a clear relation of the river to the mill, and the mill to the village. The dam is visible upstream, and the background fades into western Alamance County toward the mill villages of Altamahaw and Ossipee. The company store is at the intersection of the two roads at right. The race is particularly clear. It is the narrow strip of water that flows next to the mill, creating an island to the left. The water from that race flowed into the power plant and was used to generate the power necessary to operate the mill's equipment. After 1880, new mills turned to steam for power, and even Glencoe and the older mills on the river converted to steam by 1913. (THM.)

THE GLENCOE COTTON MILLS, W. E. & J. H. HOLT, PROPRIETORS, NEAR BURLINGTON, N. C.

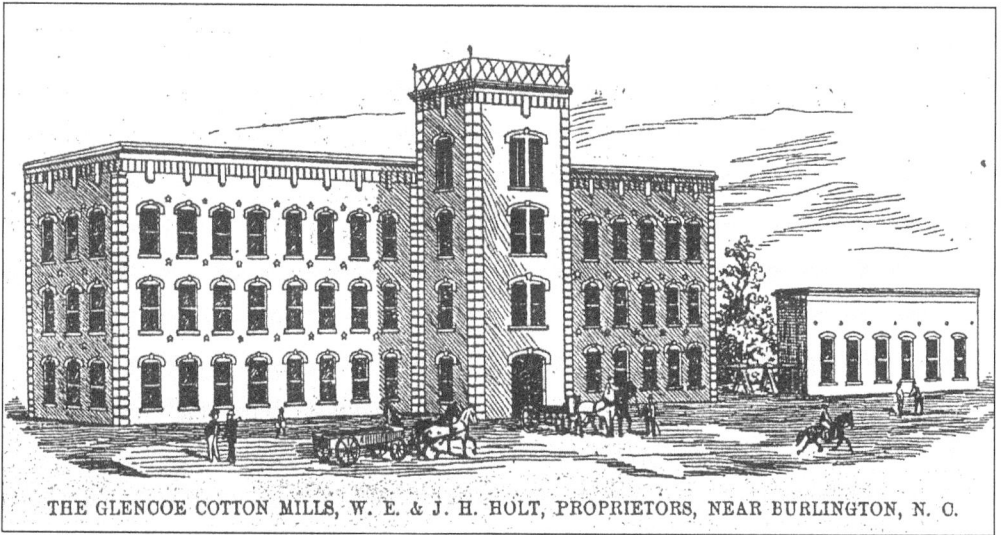

This drawing advertised Glencoe Mill a few years after it was organized in Alamance County, North Carolina, in 1880. The new mill had been built on the banks of the Haw River. J.H. and W.E. Holt, the proprietors, were sons of E.M. Holt, who had built a mill in 1837 at Alamance and later pioneered dyed fabric in the Southern United States. (THM.)

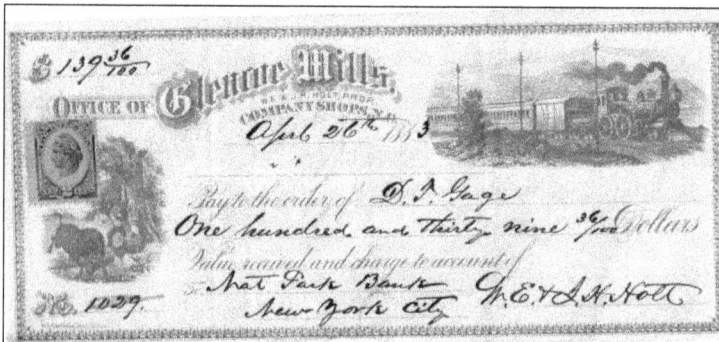

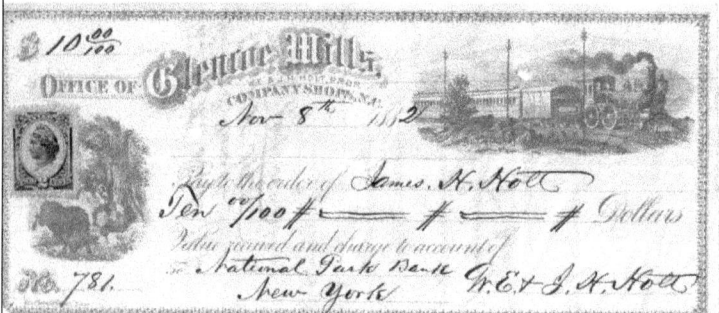

These checks were written by officials of Glencoe Mill during its early existence, in 1882 and 1883, and the address is listed as Company Shops. That was a railroad town, home of repair facilities for the North Carolina Railroad. In 1887, the town's name was changed to Burlington. W.E. Holt and Robert L. Holt signed both. (THM.)

14

Graham, N.C. Nov 7th 18__

Mesr W.E. & J.H. Holt

BOUGHT OF E. M. HOLT'S SONS,

SUCCESSORS TO E.M.HOLT.

MANUFACTURERS OF

ALAMANCE PLAIDS

THE CALVERT LITH. CO. DETROIT.

J.H. HOLT.
W.E. HOLT.
L.H. HOLT.
J.N. WILLIAMSON.
LAWRENCE S. HOLT

ESTABLISHED 1837

S: Plaids 60 days.
1% 30 days or 2% for Cash.
S 30 days less 1% for Cash.

Cottonades, Ticks, Drills, Shirtings, Cotton Yarns

20 Sacks Flour   237½   47.50

This was an 1884 order form for E.M. Holt's Sons. Noted under the name is that this was previously E.M. Holt and Sons, but in 1884 E.M. Holt was dead, so the company reorganized to include sons J.H. Holt, W.E. Holt, L.H. Holt, Lawrence S. Holt, and son-in-law J.N. Williamson. By 1884, the Holt family was involved in a number of mills in Alamance County. There was the original mill at Alamance. Another was located at Bellemont, one at Carolina, as well as the one at Glencoe. The family was also involved in the mills at Ossipee, Haw River, and Saxapahaw. This order form did not list the name of either of the mills in which the family was involved. Therefore, it appeared that E.M. Holt's Sons was a sales organization for several or perhaps all of the mills. (THM.)

Glencoe Mill was a cotton mill. It took raw cotton and spun it and eventually turned it into fabric that was sent off to the markets. Trucks brought cotton to the mill door, and workers took it from there to begin the production process. It was not until the 1920s that some cotton mills turned to a new material—rayon. (THM.)

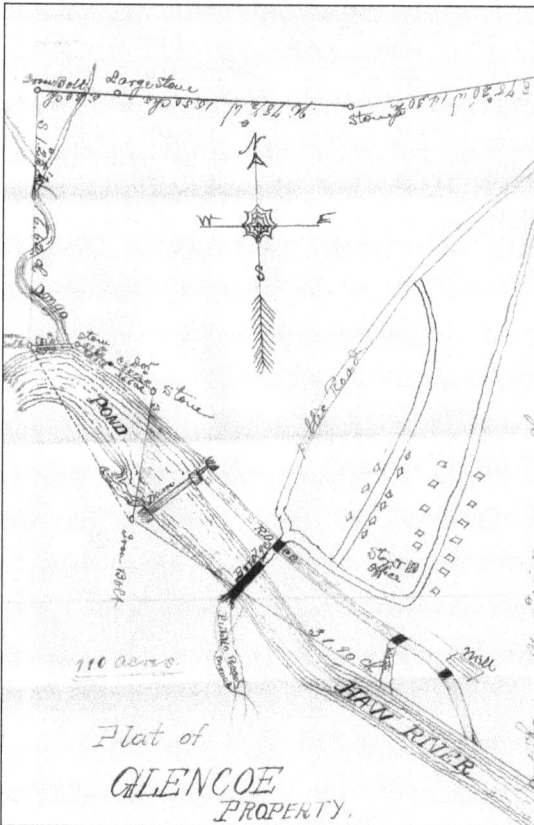

This plat of the Glencoe Mill and its village, dated May 18, 1899, shows the mill site in relation to both the river and the mill village. The property comprised 110 acres. The dam is marked in the river with what was called a "pond" behind it. (THM.)

Glencoe Mill village formed a thriving community in 1918. The road runs up to the office building and company store, and off to the right of that structure is where the employee houses were located. To the left of the flagpole is a well in front of the mill. The water tower at right remains in place today. (THM.)

C.R. Moffitt is shown here at work in the Glencoe Mill about 1900. Hours in the mill were long. In the early days, workers had 12-hour days, six days a week. Often, they went to work in the dark and went home in the dark at the end of the shift. (THM.)

James H. Holt Jr. joined his father in the Glencoe Mill. In 1890, James Jr. and his brother Robert left Glencoe to form Windsor Cotton Mill in Burlington. After the death of James Holt Sr. in 1897, James Jr. moved to the Lakeside Mill to help his brother William in that operation. James died in 1928. (THM.)

This charming young lady is Margaret Elizabeth Holt, the daughter of James Henry Holt Jr. and Olive Joyner Holt. James Holt's father was the son of E.M. Holt, who started the Holt textile empire in his mill at Alamance. Margaret, the youngest of the Holts' four children, was born in 1908. (THM.)

On December 12, 1929, Margaret Elizabeth Holt was married to Walter Monroe Brown Jr. Margaret was 21 years old at the time of her marriage. This is her formal wedding portrait, showing the beautiful gown she chose for the ceremony. It seemed fitting that such a beautiful dress would be chosen for the daughter of a textile manufacturer. Margaret and Walter had three children, Elizabeth Hood Brown, Walter Monroe Brown III, and Margaret Holt Brown. Although Margaret had three siblings, none lived beyond seven years of age. The first child, a girl, died in infancy in 1902. James Henry Holt III died at two months old the next year. Olive Farish Holt was born in 1904 and died in 1911. Margaret was the fourth of those children. Margaret's father, James Henry Holt Jr., had died a year before her marriage. (THM.)

There is no date on this photograph of the workers at Glencoe Mill, but some place it around 1900. Standing at left is George Washington Murray, a member of one of the early families in Glencoe. Murray was a superintendent in the plant. As was the case in most mills at that time, there are the old, the very young, male, and female among the workforce. In early years of the

mill's operations, employees worked 12-hour days, six days per week. Sunday was the only day off. There were holidays, however, when dry weather lowered the river level so much that there was not enough river flow for the generation of power. (THM.)

The Marshall family had several members who worked in the Glencoe Mill. Seen here on their porch in the village is Mary Elizabeth (left), holding a child. From left to right are (first row) an unidentified person, Ed, Carl, Florene, and an unidentified person; (second row) Dorothy, Ida, Minnie Marshall Hurley, Kate, Argie Marshall Atkins, and Ethel Marshall Faucette. (THM.)

Mary Elizabeth Marshall is seated here with the girls in the Marshall family. Ida is standing behind, with Minnie to her side. In front are, from left to right, Dorothy, Argie, and Florence. The Marshalls were another large family with many members working in Glencoe Mill. The family lived on the lower end of Back Street. (THM.)

Glencoe Mill employees pause from their work in 1895 to pose in front of the building. By this time, Glencoe Mill had taken its place as a key player in the economic life of Alamance County. The textile industry was the lifeblood of the county in those years, with many mills in operation. (THM.)

Holt's Glencoe Plaids were well known in the textile industry when Glencoe Mill was in full production. Holt plaids had their beginning at E.M. Holt's Alamance Mill in 1853, when a Frenchman taught the workers how to dye their yarn. Holt produced the first commercially dyed material in the South, a move that launched a textile dynasty in Alamance. (THM.)

James Waddell was a young man when he went to work for Glencoe Mill in 1916. He operated the company store, a position he held for almost 30 years. He also had a role in distributing the wages. Payroll was delivered to his store on Wednesday afternoons, and he distributed the money to employees on Thursdays. (THM.)

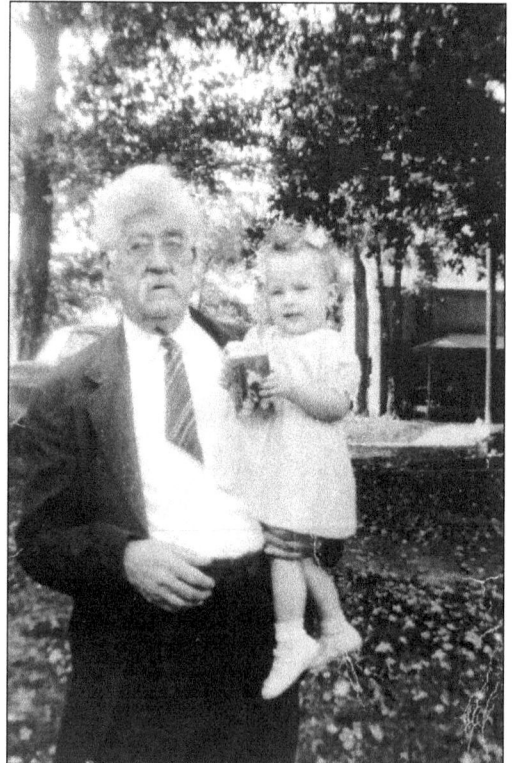

James Waddell was for many years the operator of the company store at Glencoe Mill. He is shown here holding his little granddaughter Brenda Shell. Waddell kept the store open long hours, Monday through Saturday. On Wednesday nights, he slept in the store with his gun, as the mill payroll was there for payment on Thursday. (Courtesy of Jean Lassiter.)

Louisa, one of the James Waddell children, is shown here with a smaller, unidentified child. The house behind, apparently the Waddell home, looks quite neat and well kept. The automobile appears to be one of the old touring cars, with a fabric top that folded down for open riding. (Courtesy of Jean Lassiter.)

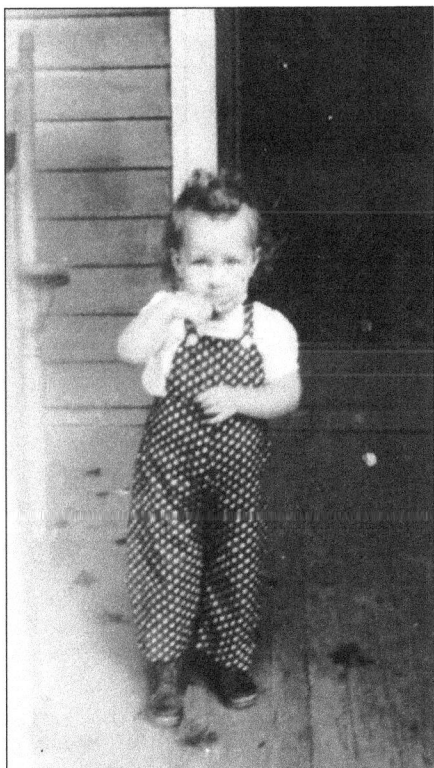

Little Brenda Shell was one of a number of children and grandchildren who were in and out of the James Waddell home in the mill village. She was a granddaughter. The Waddell home was a mill house across the street from the company store that James Waddell operated for the mill. (Courtesy of Jean Lassiter.)

Mr. and Mrs. James Waddell were part of Glencoe history for many years. He joined the company in 1916 and operated the store for 30 years. He opened at 6:30 a.m. each day and closed at 9:00 p.m. An assistant came to work after his shift was over to relieve Waddell for a short time each day. Waddell died in 1946. (THM.)

The Glencoe Mill company store was one of the most important operations in the community. Workers and their families depended on the store for most of their supplies. James Waddell operated the store from 1916 into the 1940s, and it was here on Thursdays that workers received their pay for the week. (THM.)

This is a view of the interior of the company store. This photograph shows the back section of the store. It was here that various over-the-counter medical products were sold, such as pain relievers and medications for a cold. Included were a lot of patent medicines of the time. (THM.)

George T. Faucette, his wife, and the family cat pose on the porch of their Glencoe home. The Faucettes, like everyone else in the village, lived a simple life. They worked long hours in the mill, had a few hours at home when the day was over, went to the company store, and then went back to work the next morning. Sunday was the day for church and visiting. (THM.)

In this 1922 photograph, Jesse Swain rides in a goat-powered wagon belonging to John Cook. The wagon was used by Cook to help him care for an invalid son, Jeffrey. Jesse Swain was born in Glencoe. The Blue Grass Coaster looks like an efficient mode of transportation. It even has a brake handle over the word "Blue." (THM.)

In the early 1900s, three more members of the Marshall family visited a studio to pose for a photograph. Seen here are, from left to right, Dorothy, Minnie, and Florene. These girls grew up in Glencoe village. Younger ones would have gone to the old Glencoe School just north of the village, while the older ones were more likely to go to work at the mill rather than attend school. (THM.)

Osborne Hughes Phillips holds his grandson George M. Phillips Jr. in this photograph taken in the Glencoe village not long after little George was born in 1930. George Jr. was the 10th of 11 children born to George Madison Phillips and Eva Pennington Phillips. The Phillips family had three generations live and work in Glencoe. Osborne Phillips represents the first generation, and George Jr. represents the third. Osborne Phillips was an honored and respected member of Glencoe Methodist Church for many years, and the bell from that church now sits in his honor in front of St. Luke's Methodist Church, a short distance from Glencoe. The 10 siblings of George Jr. have all died, leaving him as the sole survivor of the big family. He now serves as pastor of a church just a few miles from Glencoe. (THM.)

This is an older generation of the Phillips family. They are children of Joel Madison Phillips and Rebecca Turner Philips. Shown here are, from left to right, (first row) Minnie Crawford, Betsy Ann Shaw, Nancy May, and Martha Euliss; (second row) Charlie, William, George Luther, Osborne, and James Levi Phillips. (THM.)

George Madison Phillips and his wife, Eva May Pennington Phillips, are shown in a portrait in the early 1900s. They were married on October 13, 1912. They lived in the Glencoe village for many years and reared a family of seven girls and four sons, several of whom worked in the mill. (THM.)

These Phillips boys, George Jr., Carey, and Billy, smile for the camera beside the well at their house in the 1930s. George is dressed up, complete with bow tie, because he was to be in a program at the Glencoe School the day this photograph was taken. (THM.)

Just over 100 members of the Glencoe Mill workforce gathered in 1913 outside the facility for a group photograph. There are men, women, and children, as entire families worked long hours together in the mill well into the 20th century, when laws began to regulate the employment of children. (THM.)

Mary Catherine Foster Durham worked and lived in Glencoe for many years. She was there in the early years of the mill. This photograph was made near the turn of the 20th century. She was typical of many women who worked alongside their husbands, and children, in the mill. (THM.)

A second photograph shows Mary Catherine Foster Durham in the later years of her life. She lived in the village most of her life and worked until no longer able. She was skilled at sewing and was referred to by some as the "quilt lady." The Textile Heritage Museum in the village has examples of her work. (THM.)

Elizabeth Wilson had perfect attendance in the sixth grade at Glencoe School in 1914–1915. This certificate was presented to her at the end of the school year, which, at that time, was at the end of April. Glencoe School then was a frame building with two rooms. A new school replaced it in 1936. (THM.)

Alamance County Public Schools

CERTIFICATE OF HONOR FOR
REGULAR AND PROMPT ATTENDANCE

This is to Certify, That _Elizabeth Wilson_

of the _6th_ Grade, in the _Glencoe_ School,

District Number _#4_, _Faucette_ Township,

has been neither absent nor tardy during the scholastic year 19__–__ and in recognition of this regularity and punctuality is presented with this

CERTIFICATE

This _24th_ day of _April_ 19__

County Board of Education { J. L. SCOTT, S. E. TATE, J. W. WHITEHEAD

W. B. Stinson
COUNTY SUPERINTENDENT

TEACHER

No community is without its tragedies. This photograph shows the home of L. Banks Williamson at Glencoe after it had been heavily damaged by fire. Williamson was the son of John Lea Williamson and Fanny Ann Holt, a daughter of E.M. Holt. This house was located east of the mill village, near the entrance to Glencoe. (THM.)

Mill houses were simple. The front door opened into a hallway, and on the right side was a living room. On the other side of the hallway was a bedroom, and in the back was the kitchen. There were two bedrooms upstairs. In the early years, there was no electricity, no running water, and no indoor plumbing. (THM.)

This baseball team represented Glencoe in 1938. Lettering on the shirts indicate a Burlington fence company that provided sponsorship. Shown here are, from left to right, (first row) Floyd Allen (batboy); (second row) Allen Murray, Louis Fuquay, Pete Jones, Dexter Austin, Mike Rascoe, Doyle Wrenn, West Caulder; (third row) Herman Webster, John Swain, Sammy Marshall, Chester Moore, ? Euliss, Hillary Jones, Jack Oliver, and Nathan Pennington. (Courtesy of Dexter Austin.)

34

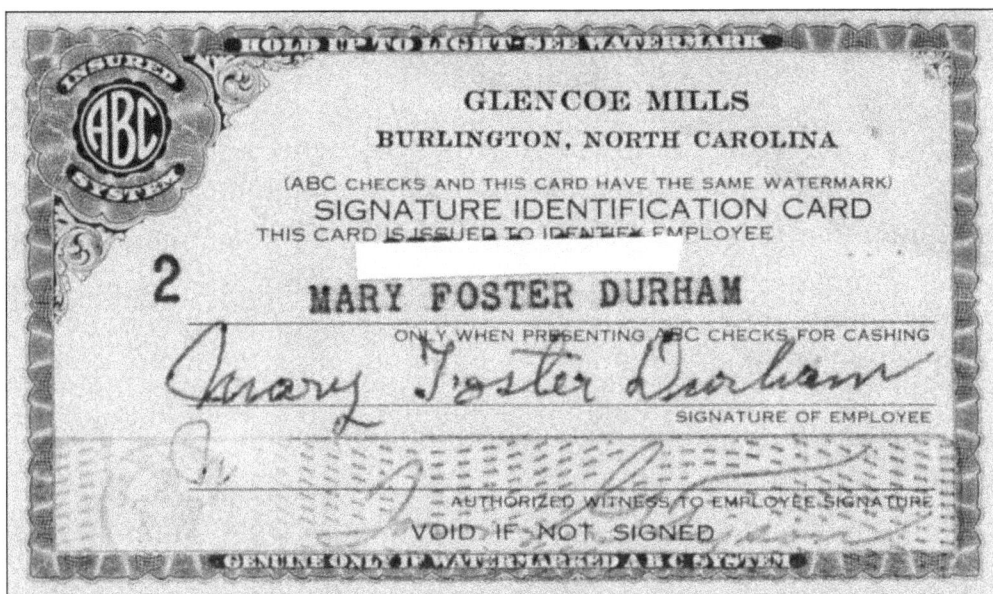

Employees at Glencoe Mill were issued a special identification card. Information on the card states that it was to be used for the cashing of checks. This card was issued to Mary Foster Durham, a longtime employee at Glencoe. Precautions were taken, including watermarks on the card, to prevent someone from making a copy. (THM.)

Nancy Imogene Phillips (left) and her sister Erma Dell Phillips (right) enjoyed a snowstorm that hit the Glencoe village about 1950. Winter made things difficult for residents, as they depended on wells for water, and these wells could freeze in winter. A trip to the outhouse was a pretty cold adventure as well. (THM.)

Erma Dell (left) and Helen Phillips (center) are shown here with Ruth Wyrick (right) and James "Dink" Holland, who was courting Helen. The couple met during World War II. He went into the Army and served in Europe. He was taken as a prisoner of war but was released at war's end and came home to marry Helen. (THM.)

Helen Phillips and James "Dink" Holland are shown after Holland's return from service in World War II. He wears ribbons for medals earned in that conflict. The couple had met in the Glencoe village just before he shipped off to Europe in July 1944, and they were married soon after his return. (THM.)

James "Dink" Holland and his wife, Helen, take a trip back in time as they swing on the front porch of the house where she lived when Holland first met her. They courted in the swing before he went off to World War II. As soon as Holland got home, he sought her out and asked her to marry him. He then went to work for Western Electric. (THM.)

"Dink" and Helen Holland pose with a model of the house in which Helen lived in the Glencoe village in the 1940s. "Dink" Holland made the house and presented it to the Textile Heritage Museum for display. Helen was one of 11 children who grew up in the mill village house. (THM.)

Shown here are, from left to right, Bryan "Bill" Holland, Ruby Nell Massey, Helen Phillips, and Charles McKinney using the steel bridge over the river at Glencoe as a backdrop for a photograph. Young people in the village were attracted to the bridge as a meeting place, and it was often the site of photographs like this one. (THM.)

Erma Dell Phillips is dressed for Mother's Day. She wears the traditional flower in honor of her mother. Behind her is a typical house in the Glencoe village, and between the pole and the right side of the photograph is one of the wells used by the residents. She married Ted Neal, and she died in 2010. (THM.)

The George Madison Phillips family remained close after leaving the Glencoe village. They often gathered for family reunions. On this occasion in 1990, seven of the 11 siblings were together. They are, from left to right, (first row) Helen, Opal, and Erma Dell; (second row) Delbert, Carey, Jack, and Billie. In 2015, Jack is the only surviving member of the family. (THM.)

Cyrus Manning Tyson was the bookkeeper and the mill superintendent at Glencoe. He lived in a house across from the company store where he had his office. Minnie Gibson Tyson was his wife, and their children were Edna and Thomas Gibson. The family is shown here in the early 20th century. (Courtesy of Tom Tyson.)

Cyrus Manning Tyson died in 1944, but he was a fixture at Glencoe Mill for many years. He worked in the company office that joined the company store. He had a son, Thomas Gibson Tyson, who later worked for the mill, and his job was in the office with his father. (Courtesy of Tom Tyson.)

The best place to beat the heat on a summer day in the Glencoe village was on the back porch. Members of the George Madison Phillips family enjoy time together here. This house was typical of those built in the village for workers and their families. They were simple framed houses with metal roofs. (THM.)

These two young ladies use the steel bridge at Glencoe for a photograph backdrop. Esper Mitchell (left) and Wynona Murray Allen (right) are dressed in their Sunday best. Here again, their clothing is in keeping with the styles of the 1930s. At that time, Glencoe was a thriving community with a mill that was running at full speed. (THM.)

Frank Swain sits on the front porch of his Glencoe home with his guitar and Jesse Swain at his side. The location of this particular mill house, however, is not certain. Some members of the family remember Swain's daughter Evie Swain saying, "We lived in so many different houses, no telling which one that was." The mill gave families the opportunity to move to a better house when someone moved out. Apparently, the Swain family was not the only one that moved about the village. Another former resident remembered his family living in five different houses. Swain's guitar was likely a good source of entertainment for the family. Some families had radios, but several residents in the village had musical skills. Some of these residents provided music at the two churches at Glencoe. (Courtesy of Patsy Pennington Harwood.)

Frank Swain holds Quincy, and his wife, Ella Horner Swain, holds their daughter Evie. Swain and his wife worked in the mill, and Evie would later work there as well. Quincy did not work there. In later years, most everyone knew Ella as "Granny." (Courtesy of Patsy Pennington Harwood.)

While the Haw River supplied water to power Glencoe Mill, it also provided recreation opportunities. Evie Pennington is shown here in a rowboat moving along the river. On the back of the photograph is written "Easter Monday, 1925." Easter Monday has long been a holiday in North Carolina. (Courtesy of Patsy Pennington Harwood.)

The Murray family was large, and several of its members worked in the mill. This young man, Allie Jasper Murray, was there in the early part of the 20th century. He was the son of Lewis Craven Murray, and he later married Mary Anne Mallessa Morene. (Courtesy of Rosalyn Sumner.)

James Henry Murray, born in 1843, was a member of the Murray family who did not work in the mill. He went to Tennessee before 1880 and did not return. His first wife, Emily Wallech, died in 1873. His second wife, Catherine Palmer, poses here with Murray. She came back to Glencoe and worked in the mill after 1900. (Courtesy of Rosalyn Sumner.)

Ernest Arnold Murray, son of James Henry and Emily Murray, is shown on the porch of his home in Glencoe with his wife, Leora, and children Carl (left), Pearl (center), and Ernest Jr. (right). Murray did well in his work in the Glencoe Mill and held positions of responsibility. Later, he left the mill for Roanoke Rapids, North Carolina, where he headed operations of a textile mill. (Courtesy of Rosalyn Sumner.)

Maggie Murray Jordan was one of a number of members of the Murray family working at Glencoe Mill around the turn of the 20th century. The 1900 and 1910 censuses show her working there as a weaver. Her husband, Thomas Lamberth Jordan, died in December 1900, but she continued to work in the mill. (Courtesy of Rosalyn Sumner.)

Maggie Murray Jordan and her family were working in Glencoe in 1900 when her husband, Thomas, died. His death meant a greater burden on his wife, who had a family to support. She did just that, continuing to work as a weaver at the mill. She is seen here with daughter Sallie Emma Jordan. (Courtesy of Rosalyn Sumner.)

Catherine Murray is listed in the 1880 census living in the household of her mother, Celia Murray. She was the sister of James Henry Murray and the daughter of Joseph Rainey Murray and Celia Danieley. Here, she poses in a studio setting typical of the late 19th century. (Courtesy of Rosalyn Sumner.)

Roscoe Murray got dressed in his best suit and hat, took his bicycle, and went to the studio for a formal photograph. Murray was born in 1881, the son of James Henry and Catherine Murray, and he married Julie Webster. He worked in the mill, along with his mother and sister. (Courtesy of Rosalyn Sumner.)

Ann Murray was another daughter of Joseph and Hannah Palmer Murray. She worked alongside her family in the Glencoe Mill for a number of years. She married Ben Shepherd. There was indeed a large number of the Murray family in Glencoe. At one time, Murrays lived on both Front and Back Streets in the village. (Courtesy of Rosalyn Sumner.)

Bessie Murray strikes a pose for a photograph that might have been a Valentine card. She was the daughter of Joseph Madkin Murray and Hannah Elizabeth Murray and another member of the family who worked in the mill. She was first married to Rufus A. Jackson and then to Harry Thomas. (Courtesy of Rosalyn Sumner.)

George Washington Murray was a supervisor in the Glencoe Mill near the turn of the 20th century. This is an unusual photograph, as it shows Murray soon after he was cured of scrofula, a disease of the lymph nodes. It appears that the photograph was made to show scars from that illness. (Courtesy of Rosalyn Sumner.)

Mary Ellen Murray was another daughter of James Henry and Catherine Murray. She came home from Tennessee in 1900 with her mother after her father died. She worked in the mill, as did her husband, Cleve Williamson. They were married in Alamance County, but they later moved to Union City, South Carolina. (Courtesy of Rosalyn Sumner.)

CHRISTMAS
GREETINGS

Wishing You a
Very Merry Christmas
and a Happy and
Prosperous New Year

Glencoe Mills

This is a nice greeting card for those employed at Glencoe Mill. Wishes for a merry Christmas and a prosperous new year came from the mill owners. However, this was far more than a greeting card to the workers. It was their pay envelope. Each week, workers received their pay in similar envelopes. (THM.)

William Freeland Murray and his wife, Barbara Ellen Payne Murray, did not live in the village. Their home was located across the river. Their names were found in the company store records in the early 1900s. They were married in 1887 and had three sons, two of whom became textile workers. The third was a carpenter. (THM.)

Holt Green, who operated the mill with his father, Walter, prior to World War II, works in his office in the company store building. Green became a member of the OSS. On a secret mission, he parachuted into Europe, behind enemy lines. He was captured by the Germans and executed as a spy. (THM.)

Doris Wilson Wilkerson poses in front of one of the wells that served the Glencoe Mill village. Most of the 41 houses in the village had a well, while a few residents had to share a well. Doris was the daughter of the Reverend Ralph Wilson, for many years the pastor of Glencoe Baptist Church. (THM.)

Walter Guerry Green Jr. was the last man to head Glencoe Mill. He was the son of Walter G. Green and Lelia Daisy Holt Green, daughter of James Henry Holt. Green served in the US Navy in World War II and returned to operate the mill until it closed in 1954. Green was also an attorney and an unsuccessful candidate for US Congress. (THM.)

Richard Duck was the cook and butler for the Holt family in the big owners' house. He was there for a long period of time, in the 1930s and beyond. He and his wife, Lula Belle, at one time lived in a single room attached to the store building. Later, they lived in a small home near the owner's house. (THM.)

Lula Belle Duck was the wife of Richard Duck. There is a quilt in the Textile Heritage Museum she made in 1935 from cotton feed sacks. It was entirely hand-sewn, using scraps. Long-john underwear, inserted in it for additional warmth, probably belonged to Richard. (THM.)

This is the quilt made by Lula Belle Duck and daughter Lillie Mae Duck, which now in the Textile Heritage Museum. Made in the 1930s, it is an example of how women made use of every possible item during tough times. This one was made from scraps of cotton-feed sacks and other cloth sacks they could find. (THM.)

This old building is in poor shape today, but, at one time, it was a place of much activity. It was the lodge for the Order of United American Mechanics in Glencoe. The group had a funeral benefit department, and it stood "for the public school with the American flag over it, and against any union of church and state."

One of the most interesting buildings in the Glencoe Mill village was the barbershop. It was a very small, white building on Front Street, and the familiar red-and-white-striped barber pole out front welcomed customers. This building has been restored and is an attraction today, as people have returned to restore homes and live in the village.

After the mill closed in 1954, some continued to live in the village. But as the houses fell into disrepair, most people moved out. That made the decaying process worse, as there was no one to keep up the property. One by one, the old houses were reclaimed by nature. It appeared the old village would become a victim of time. (THM.)

When Tom Hanford worked for Preservation North Carolina on the Glencoe project, much of the property looked like the building behind him here. In his work from 1963 to 2010, he saw the area declared a National Historic Site. He also saw property sold to private individuals, restorations undertaken, and the village of Glencoe reborn. (THM.)

Glencoe School was constructed in 1936 to replace the original small frame building. A Public Works Administration project for the Alamance County Schools, it had six rooms until it was enlarged in 1951 to include a cafeteria and kitchen. It closed in 1961. The school was listed as a National Historic Site in 2010.

Glencoe Methodist Church stood about halfway between the mill and the upper end of Front Street. This building was erected in 1898 by the mill as Union Church, serving all denominations. Both Methodists and Baptists worshipped there for a number of years. The Baptists moved out in 1914, when their new Glencoe Baptist Church was erected. The Methodists stayed for many years. By 1959, the condition of the old building was so bad that it was deemed beyond repair, and the village was in a state of decline. Land was purchased in the Green Acres area on Greenwood Drive. The congregation moved to the old Glencoe School for services while the new church was under construction. The first unit was completed in 1964, and the sanctuary was opened in 1979. St. Luke's United Methodist Church is located a short distance west of the Glencoe village. This old building was finally torn down in 1976. (THM.)

Glencoe Baptist Church was formed in 1893. At first, members had to meet in the old gristmill building, as there were no other facilities available. A few years later, the mill constructed a church building in the middle of the village and made it available to all denominations as Union Church. The Baptists met there as they became more firmly established as a church body. They had the help of First Baptist Church in Burlington. Ministers of that church came to Glencoe on a regular basis and held services. With guidance from the Burlington church, the Glencoe members made plans for their own sanctuary. This facility was constructed in 1914, but the building had been remodeled at the time of this photograph. Later, the church was bricked and remodeled, and additions were built. It continues in use today. (Courtesy of Glencoe Baptist Church.)

In December 1893, Rev. Alvis Andrews was called by Glencoe Baptist Church as its first pastor. He remained pastor of the young church until 1896. The pastors of Burlington's First Baptist Church also filled the pulpit of Glencoe Baptist Church on a regular basis during the early years of the young church's existence. (Courtesy of Glencoe Baptist Church.)

A group of women pose for a photograph beside their church in the early 1900s. The only person identified is Mary Lester Durham, at left in the first row, holding a large frame. This photograph was made beside the Methodist church. Until 1914, both Baptists and Methodists met in that building, then called Union Church. (THM.)

Rev. Ralph Wilson (far left) leads the Glencoe Baptist Church congregation in a baptism service at the edge of the Haw River. The two men at center are holding a small girl, Thelma Massey. She and one brother were handicapped and could not walk, while a second brother was less affected. She was an accomplished musician, as was one of her brothers. (THM.)

These young men were members of Boy Scout Troop 44 in Glencoe in 1944. They are, from left to right, (first row) unidentified, Coleman Woody, Jack Phillips, unidentified, and Tom Woody; (second row) Billie Phillips,? Ross, Holt Faucette, and unidentified. Some of the members lived in the mill village, but others came from the surrounding area. (THM.)

These men pose beside the Methodist church that served the community for more than 50 years. Glencoe Methodist Church was in the middle of the village, and, when that area began to decline after the mill closed, the church found it necessary to move. The congregation eventually became St. Luke's Untied Methodist Church on Greenwood Drive. (THM.)

These women gather next to their church building, Glencoe Methodist Church, probably in the 1920s. The style of the women's clothing, especially their hats, is typical of that era. (THM.)

Gabriel and Minnie Fonville, brother and sister, gave a large donation to the Glencoe Baptist Church to be applied to the construction of a new building. Glencoe Mill gave funds for the new sanctuary, which was completed in 1914. Prior to that time, the congregation had met in the old Union Church. (Courtesy of Glencoe Baptist Church.)

By 1994, Glencoe Baptist Church had undergone a number of renovations and expansions. The church was bricked, an education building was added, and a fellowship hall was constructed behind the church. In addition, a cross was added to the original structure. The latest expansion involved construction of a worship center across the street from the sanctuary.

Rev. Thad McDonald was pastor of Glencoe Methodist Church in 1944. He is shown here on Easter Sunday in that year, standing on the steel bridge over the river. The Methodist church, located in the middle of the village, had an active congregation during years when the mill operated. (THM.)

By 1953, W.M. Wilkins, 75, had worked at Glencoe Mill for 55 years, the oldest employee in years of service. He had perfect attendance since 1911, and he and Mrs. Wilkins had lived in the same mill house since they were married in 1900. He was a beam warper at the mill. (THM.)

This was the situation facing the people who came up with the idea of restoring the Glencoe Mill village. Some houses had long been vacant and were in severe disrepair. To many, it seemed a hopeless cause, but not to Sarah Rhyne. She obtained National Historic Site recognition and planted the seeds of restoration, giving Glencoe new life. (THM.)

The Glencoe owner's house is seen following complete renovation of the building and property surrounding it. In the woods to the right was a small white house where Richard Duck and his wife lived. Richard was the butler and cook for the Holts. The chauffeur lived in one of the homes behind the big house. (THM.)

The mill owner's house was located on the road that ran by the village between Burlington and Caswell County. It was set apart from the homes of the workers by a green area and a grove of trees. The last of the owners to live there was Walter Green Jr. After his death, the house was uncared for and fell into a state of severe disrepair (above). As the effort began to restore the Glencoe Mill village, George and Jerrie Nall bought the property and undertook a massive renovation of the old house (below). Not only was the house restored, but furnishings of the type the Holt family would have used were placed throughout the house. (Both, THM.)

George and Jerrie Nall stand in the elaborate dining room of the Glencoe Mill owner's house. The Nalls bought the house several years ago and restored it to its original beauty. They also furnished the house with antiques of the period when the Holt family occupied it. (THM.)

This bedroom in the owner's house at Glencoe looks as it might have when the Holts lived there. There is a tea set on the bed, and shoes are at the bedside. Jerrie and George Nall went to great lengths to restore the house to its original state, in keeping with the restoration of the houses in which the mill workers lived. (THM.)

This quiet scene shows buildings in the village that have been renovated and now are used by new residents. After falling into decline over several years, family dwellings and outbuildings such as this one are being restored. Through the bare trees, other houses are visible on another street. (THM.)

Many of the old mill houses have been renovated and brought into the modern era by their new owners. This house has been remodeled to have one side of the rear section dominated by windows. The sun always hits the house on this side, providing not only a bright room, but also adding heat during the winter.

The mill constructed both one-story and two-story houses for its workers. This one on Back Street is one of the smaller houses that has been totally refurbished and is now occupied. It has been neatly restored with a new metal roof, and the chimney has been restored to new condition. Many of the village houses were in shambles before the effort was started to revive Glencoe. Years without maintenance meant windows were broken, roofs were in disrepair, and some houses needed new foundation support. In the old village, one-story houses were just alike as were the two-storied units. New owners have sought individuality, and houses now have additions, and varied colors have been chosen. The colors add not only individuality, but a drastic change from the drab houses in the past. Of course, there have been updates in plumbing and electricity.

St. Luke's United Methodist Church is located on Greenwood Drive, a short distance west of Glencoe. It grew from the Methodist church in the mill village that initially was Union Church, where Baptist and Methodist groups met. The Baptists built their own church in 1914, and the Methodists continued there until the late 1950s.

Ann Hobgood was the first person to buy and restore one of the Glencoe Mill houses. She moved into the village in 1999 and was there for two years before another resident came. She has become acquainted with residents from the past and has attended their reunions and received firsthand information about life in the old village.

Two

The Haw River
Cradle for Textiles and Politics

The Haw River was a vital resource for the Indians who lived in present-day Alamance County so many years ago. It was their major source of fish, drinking water, and other necessities. Later, after the Indians moved on and European settlers came into the area, the river continued to serve those same needs. But in the 19th century, it took on a new life. It became the cradle in which the textile industry was nurtured in Piedmont North Carolina.

E.M. Holt built a mill on Great Alamance Creek in 1837. In 1853, he began producing the first colored cloth in the South, and a textile dynasty was born. His sons followed him, building mills at Bellemont, just below Alamance, and then at Carolina and Glencoe on Haw River. There was a mill at Saxapahaw, and new mills sprang up at Ossipee, Altamahaw, Carolina, Hopedale, Haw River, and Swepsonville—all on Haw River. The rushing water was used to generate power to operate looms. Glencoe Mill, opened in 1880, was the last mill to be located on the river. New sources of power made operations possible in other locations. Not only did the river birth the textile industry, but its banks proved fertile ground for politicians who impacted state and national history. Thomas M. Holt, E.M. Holt's son and operator of the Haw River Mill, entered state politics with election to the general assembly. He was elected lieutenant governor in 1888, and, when Gov. Daniel Fowle died two years into the term, Holt became governor, serving two years. He did not seek reelection.

A Haw River dairy farmer and state agriculture commissioner, W. Kerr Scott was elected governor in 1948 and later was elected to the US Senate. His son Robert W. Scott was elected governor in 1968. Kerr Scott died in office while in the Senate and was succeeded by B. Everett Jordan, who operated the mill at Saxapahaw. He served until 1972.

Although not located on the Haw River, this mill served as an incubator for some that were there. E.M. Holt opened this mill on Alamance Creek in 1837. Years later, the mill began producing colored fabric, the first mill in the South to do so. Holt and his sons then began opening other mills, turning to Haw River as a power source.

James M. Williamson of the E.M. Holt family built the Ossipee Cotton Mill in 1878. Ossipee is across the river from the first Glen Raven Mill. The mill evolved through several owners, until it became a part of Burlington Mills. Here, Ossipee workers gather in the 1930s. J.C. Cowan, mill superintendent, is in the first row, ninth from right. He later became president of Burlington Industries.

In 1880, just upstream from Glencoe, Glen Raven Mills was born. John Q. Gant and Berry Davidson built a textile factory at the site of a gristmill. Davidson later left, and Gant built Glen Raven into a company that today has plants in China and France and is the leader in awning fabrics, under the Sunbrella name. This was the first office building at what is now Altamahaw.

A mile downstream from Glencoe, James H. Holt and other members of the E.M. Holt family built the Carolina Cotton Mill in 1867. James H., W.E., L. Banks Holt, and J.N. Williamson were involved, and in 1873, Lawrence Holt joined the group. It was James who, in 1880, decided to begin the mill at Glencoe.

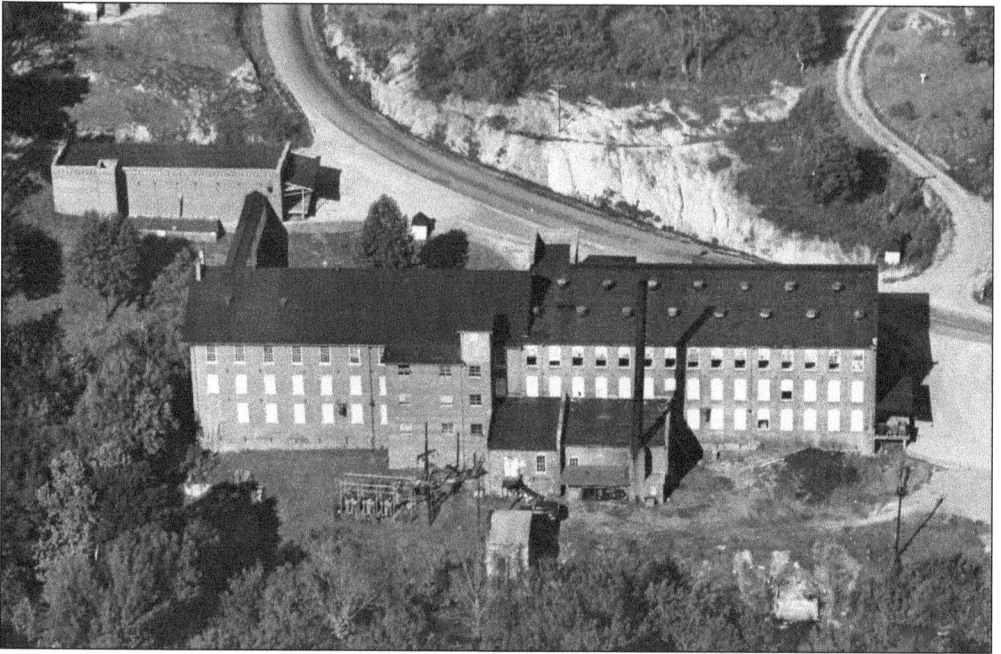

Carolina Cotton Mill was another of the several textile mills that drew its life from the Haw River. It sat on the river's edge, the race running three quarters of a mile up the river. There was a company store and a village of mill houses for employees. Carolina Mill operated for more than 100 years.

Copland Fabrics continues operations today, having been formed in 1939. John Trollinger and Jesse Gant built Highfalls Manufacturing Co. in 1832, less than a mile south of Carolina Mill. The mill went through several owners and community names until 1939, when it was opened by a group headed by J.R. Copland. By then, the name of the community was Hopedale.

Downstream from Hopedale is the town of Haw River, a community that dates to 1747. Benjamin Trollinger built a mill there in 1844 and sold to E.M. Holt and Thomas M. Holt in 1858. This is Haw River near the turn of the 20th century. The big brick building was the original site of a gristmill. Mill operations here later became a part of Cone Mills. The North Carolina Railroad crosses the Haw River at this point, connecting eastern and western North Carolina. Benjamin Trollinger built a railroad bridge here and one to the east to entice the railroad company to build the line through Alamance County. He also helped develop a land site just to the west of Haw River that would become the site of the railroad's repair and maintenance shops. That location later became Burlington. Without his efforts, the tracks might have bypassed Alamance County.

George Swepson, president of the North Carolina Railroad, built a textile mill in 1868, south of the town of Haw River. Cotton for the factory was shipped by train to Haw River, then moved downstream on barges to the mill. Textile products went the other way. The mill was last known as Virginia Mills.

The final Alamance County mill along Haw River was at Saxapahaw, although it was one of the first built on the river. John Newlin and his sons began production in 1848. E.M. Holt later owned the mill, which was operated by his sons-in-law John Lee Williamson and James White as Holt, White & Williamson.

The Saxapahaw Mill went into receivership prior to the Great Depression and was bought in 1927 by a group headed by B. Everett Jordan. The mill became Sellers Manufacturing, named for company president Charles V. Sellers. This was one of the first companies to produce high-quality silk products for the hosiery industry. Seen here is the old store and office building. (Courtesy of the *Burlington Times-News*.)

E.M. Holt died in 1884, just about the time some of his sons opened a mill near Company Shops, a railroad town that became Burlington. E.M. Holt Plaid Mill received power from a steam engine fired by wood. Lafayette Mill had opened in 1881 in Company Shops and was the first mill in the area to use steam. Lafayette later became known as Aurora Cotton Mill.

By 1879, the textile industry was in full swing along Haw River, but two of E.M. Holt's sons, Lawrence and Banks, moved to Great Alamance Creek, just south of their father's first mill. They built Bellemont Mill village, just like those along Haw River. The mill came to ruin, but the mill houses are now privately owned and form an attractive village.

In 1886, Walter and Edwin Holt, sons of Glencoe's James H. Holt, started Elmira Mill in Company Shops. This new mill was also powered by steam. New mills used a Corliss steam engine, which was fired with wood. In 1895, the mills switched from wood to coal to fuel the steam engines.

The Holt sons moved about a bit in their mill operations. James Jr. and Robert Holt left Glencoe Mill in 1890 to form Windsor Cotton Mill. Sam and William Holt took over the operations of the plant two years later. The facility, known as Lakeside Mill, is seen here.

The textile legacy of the Haw River had a major impact on Alamance County. The area continued to attract new companies. In 1923, J. Spencer Love came from Gastonia to form a new textile company. Burlington Mills was born, and it would change the textile history of the world by making products with a new synthetic fiber, rayon.

J. Spencer Love started Burlington Mills in 1923 with support from the Burlington Chamber of Commerce. Economic problems soon hit the cotton industry, so Love began producing goods made from rayon. Rayon was a huge success, and the company quickly began expanding. It would become the largest maker of textile goods in the world.

While textile mills were the primary product of the Haw River, another phenomenon was emerging along the river—the politician. Those textile mills began in the E.M. Holt family, and so did the politicians. Holt's son Thomas (pictured) entered state politics. He served in the legislature and then became North Carolina's lieutenant governor. In 1891, he became governor when the incumbent died.

Kerr Scott was not a mill man, but he was a Haw River man. A farmer, he was elected agriculture commissioner. In 1948, he was elected governor of North Carolina. Farmers played a big role in his election, and he returned the favor by improving rural roads. The "Squire of Haw River" was elected to the US Senate in 1954.

During the political career of W. Kerr Scott, big barbecue gatherings were often held at his home near the banks of Haw River. Political figures and people from all walks of life showed up. On this occasion, Scott (center) chats with Kay Kyser (left). Kyser was one of the nation's most popular bandleaders at the time.

B. Everett Jordan operated the mill at Saxapahaw and was also a major player in state politics. In 1958, he was appointed US senator when Kerr Scott died in office. He served until 1972. As chairman of the Senate Rules Committee, he directed the inauguration for Pres. Lyndon B. Johnson in 1965.

Robert W. Scott, the son of governor and senator W. Kerr Scott, himself became North Carolina's governor in 1968. During the younger Scott's administration, the consolidated University of North Carolina was formed, and the state launched its community college system. Scott later was president of that system.

Three

THE HAW RIVER
NEW LIFE FOR AN OLD STREAM

Glencoe Mill used the Haw River as it source of power when the mill opened in 1880, like several other mills along the river's 110-mile course. English explorer John Lawson visited what is now Alamance County in 1700 and in 1709 published *A New Voyage to Carolina*, in which he referenced the "Hau" river. The name comes from the Sissipahaw or Saxapahaw Indians, who lived in the area. The Haw River rises in Forsyth County in Piedmont North Carolina and flows into southern Rockingham County, across Guilford, into Alamance County near the village of Ossipee. It crosses to Glencoe, south through Carolina, Haw River, Swepsonville, and Saxapahaw before flowing into Chatham County and the Jordan Reservoir. It then runs into the Cape Fear River and on to the Atlantic Ocean. When textile mills began to appear in Carolina in the early 1800s, waters of the Haw River were used to power mill operations. Mills appeared every few miles along the way. Most operated into the mid-1900s, but some closed, as many textile operations moved overseas. Copland Fabrics and Glen Raven, however, are local companies that continue to be major operators in the world textile market. Both were born on the river.

While providing jobs for local residents, mills were adding to the pollution of the river, and by the mid-1950s, it was in bad shape. Groups formed to clean up the river, and it is again a place for town water supplies and recreation areas. There are trails for hiking and a state park at Browns Summit, near the river's source. A business in Saxapahaw provides canoes and kayaks for river adventures. There are several golf courses along its banks as well. The land along the Haw River is home to several vineyards and wineries, and there is a Haw River Wine Trail for those who savor Carolina's wines.

The Haw River is normally a quiet, meandering stream. Hurricanes, however, make it a deadly torrent of water. This flood occurred in the early 20th century. The bridge in the town of Haw River has been twice replaced. The mill in the background was once operated by Thomas M. Holt, son of E.M. Holt and once governor of North Carolina.

The dam that served the Glencoe Mill for many years remains intact across Haw River just west of the mill. Glencoe Mill opened in 1880, and early dams were either replaced or washed out in floods. The mill closed in 1954, and today, the dam is merely a pleasant scene for hikers.

The flood of 1945 put Haw River far out of its banks, and at Swepsonville a crowd gathered to watch as the waters almost touched the bottom of the steel bridge. It is at Swepsonville below this bridge that Great Alamance Creek joins the Haw River and flows on to Saxapahaw. For many years this bridge connected Swepsonville to Graham. There was a ford near this site, and it was said to have been used by Indians and other early travelers. At the end of the Civil War, a column of Confederate troops crossed here on the way to Virginia. Stories of that crossing tell of bedraggled and hungry troops plodding along. There were so many, it was stated, that it took 36 hours for the column of troops to cross the Haw River. A new bridge just north of this structure now carries traffic over the river.

Spectators who gathered at the Swepsonville bridge in 1945 were concerned that the big structure might be swept away. The bridge, however, survived without damage. The five-span steel bridge was typical of those across Alamance County until the latter years of the 20th century. All the steel bridges have now been replaced.

This aerial photograph of the Saxapahaw community shows the Haw River as it flows past the village toward Chatham County. The dam remains in place today, but the village now has such things as loft dwellings, a restaurant, a large event hall, and a country store. No longer a power source, the river is a recreation site at Saxapahaw. (Courtesy of the Burlington Times-News.)

Members of the Saxapahaw Methodist Church could have used a boat to get to church in the autumn of 1947. A storm sent the Haw River roaring out of its banks all along its course. Saxapahaw was hit hard. All the water that poured into the river along its course sent the river to its highest level in Alamance's southernmost village.

A high bridge has carried North Carolina's main east-west railroad across the Haw River at the town of the same name since the mid-1800s. That bridge has been the scene of several major train wrecks over the years, with railcars littering the river. This one occurred on November 30, 1911.

In July 1962, four Alamance County men made a voyage down the Haw River to Carolina Beach. Herman Johnson (left), Ray Maness (center), and Billy Watkins (right) made the trip with Jerry Maness (not pictured). This was before Jordan Lake was developed, and they were able to navigate the Haw River into the Cape Fear River to the beach. (Courtesy of Herman Johnson.)

Herman Johnson, Billy Watkins, and Ray and Jerry Maness reached Carolina Beach on July 6, 1962, after a trip down the Haw River. They are shown meeting friends as they docked at the beach to end the trip. They undertook the seven-day trip just for the adventure. (Courtesy of Herman Johnson.)

Herman Johnson (left) made another trip down the Haw River in May 1974. This time, he had his brother Harold (right) as part of his crew. They are shown here unloading their vessel on May 26, after they completed their trip to the coast. The journey took three days less than the 1962 trip. (Courtesy of Herman Johnson.)

New life has come to the Haw River in recent years. It is now a major attraction for those who like to paddle in a canoe or other small vessel. This map at Glencoe shows the Alamance section of the Haw River Paddle Trail. There is an access area just below the old mill, and the map shows communities all along its route, along with other access locations.

Hikers enjoy the river today as they walk the Haw River Trail, a part of the North Carolina Mountains to the Sea Trail that stretches from Clingman's Peak to the Outer Banks. This group of Friends of the North Carolina Mountains to the Sea Trail is preparing for a hike from Glencoe to neighboring Carolina. They are checking the map at the Glencoe gazebo.

The sign notes that Carolina Mill is only nine/tenths of a mile down the river as the hikers move off. This section of the trail is cared for by the recreation departments of both Burlington and Alamance County. A trail has been cleared, and there are small bridges over gullies and sets of steps up steep rises to make the journey feasible even to the most inexperienced hiker.

Much of the Haw River trail runs alongside the river, giving hikers a good view of the water and the wildlife that inhabits it. This spot is only a few steps from a major highway, but it is so secluded and quiet, hikers might feel they are miles from civilization. This is one of the feelings that make hiking the trail so attractive.

Hikers walk out of the woods as they arrive at the site that was once home to Carolina Mill. The village of Carolina is just south of Glencoe, and the Holts built a mill there more than a decade before Glencoe was opened. This section of trail runs on to the old City Lake, which was Burlington's first municipal water source.

West of the Glencoe Mill and village, the Haw River flows through woodlands and fields and along a golf course. Trees border the river and give a show of color when autumn arrives. This area has abundant wildlife, including blue herons and other birds, not to mention all the animals that live in the woods along the water.

About halfway between Indian Valley Golf Course and Glencoe village is Great Bend Park. It is a beautiful spot, accessed by the Haw River Trail and from a roadway nearby. There is a parking lot, and visitors can walk a bit of the trail and see the river in one of its prettiest locations. In the above photograph, the Glencoe dam is barely visible through the trees, a scene that is particularly pretty in the autumn. The photograph below shows one of the bridges that are found along the Haw River Trail, making the hike a bit easier and more inviting to those who just want to take a short walk along the river. At one time, Haw River was very polluted, but efforts by many people have made it a pretty piece of nature again.

Snug Harbor was a retreat built by the Glencoe Mill owners. It was a place for entertaining, for weekend outings, and for relaxation. It sat atop a hill a short distance upstream from Glencoe, with a pretty view of the river as it flowed across Alamance County. The building was lost to fire many years ago.

Snug Harbor was located atop this hill, which overlooks hole No. 11 on the Indian Valley Golf Course, Burlington's municipal course. Adventurous golfers can climb through the woods and find the foundations and chimney of the old building still there among the trees. The old building is remembered in a nearby road name, Snug Harbor Road.

Four

GLENCOE
THE TEXTILE HERITAGE MUSEUM

In 2004, the building that once housed the Glencoe Mill office and its company store found a new life. It became a museum dedicated to Glencoe's past: the Textile Heritage Museum. Today, items in that museum tell the story of textiles, not only in Glencoe, but across the South. In the 1990s, George and Jerrie Nall purchased and began restoration of the house where the Glencoe mill owners had lived. That sparked Jerrie's interest in the mill village, and she came up with the idea of a museum. She and friend Kathy Barry actually created a "traveling trunk museum" at first. Then, in 2004, the Nalls and Dr. Sam Powell, a Burlington businessman, purchased the office and store building.

From a rundown, decaying relic, the building has been beautifully restored. Visitors encounter a collection of artifacts that bring to life the story of textiles in Glencoe Mill and the Southern United States. The company-store section of the museum contains a wide variety of semipermanent displays, showing looms, spindles, cotton in various stages of production, photographs, and other things related to the Glencoe Mill and its past. In the back is a re-creation of the company store itself. The office area of the building is used for rotating displays. Past displays have shown the use of textiles in military uniforms, quilts, and beautiful dresses from the past.

A third section of the building has displays featuring some of the mills that made Alamance County famous as a textile center. Those include Burlington Industries, Glen Raven Mills, and Copland Fabrics. Products from those mills are displayed. The museum has become a favorite place for school groups and for visitors from across the nation.

The front door that was used by hundreds of mill workers over some 75 years led them to the Glencoe Mill company store. It was there that they bought things they needed for their families and for their homes. The company store was operated by the mill, and it was there that the workers were paid. The store clerk kept a tab of expenses for each worker at the store, and when the pay envelope for each was prepared, the balance of the store account was deducted. Today, the door leads to the Textile Heritage Museum. In the museum are many displays regarding the history of the mill and its village as well as the history of Alamance County and Southern textiles. The museum, in operation since 2004, continues to grow and attract visitors.

Baseball was important in the mill villages throughout Alamance County in the 1930s and 1940s. Glencoe fielded teams and competed against others in the area. There was an especially good team in 1938. These trophies, photographs, and a catcher's mask are on display in the Textile Heritage Museum as a reminder of the history of baseball and textiles.

The museum at Glencoe is located in what was once the company store for the Glencoe Mill. Some of the things used there had remained, even in the years when the store was closed and the village all but deserted. This cash register and the scales behind it were used daily in the store when the village was thriving.

A large number of bikers participated in a race across Piedmont North Carolina on October 2, 2007, and Glencoe was a rest stop for them. They were spread up and down the streets, and this picture shows a good view of the front of the main building of the old textile plant. Groups such as this visiting the museum spread the news of Glencoe across the state. The North Carolina Mountains to the Sea Trail passes through Glencoe, and hikers often stop at the museum for a tour. Other groups, including touring antique auto clubs, often stop here. In addition, there are frequent school groups as well as students from nearby Elon University who use the museum and village as a study resource. The museum has regular hours on weekends and can be open for special groups at any time during the week. (Courtesy of the *Burlington Times-News*.)

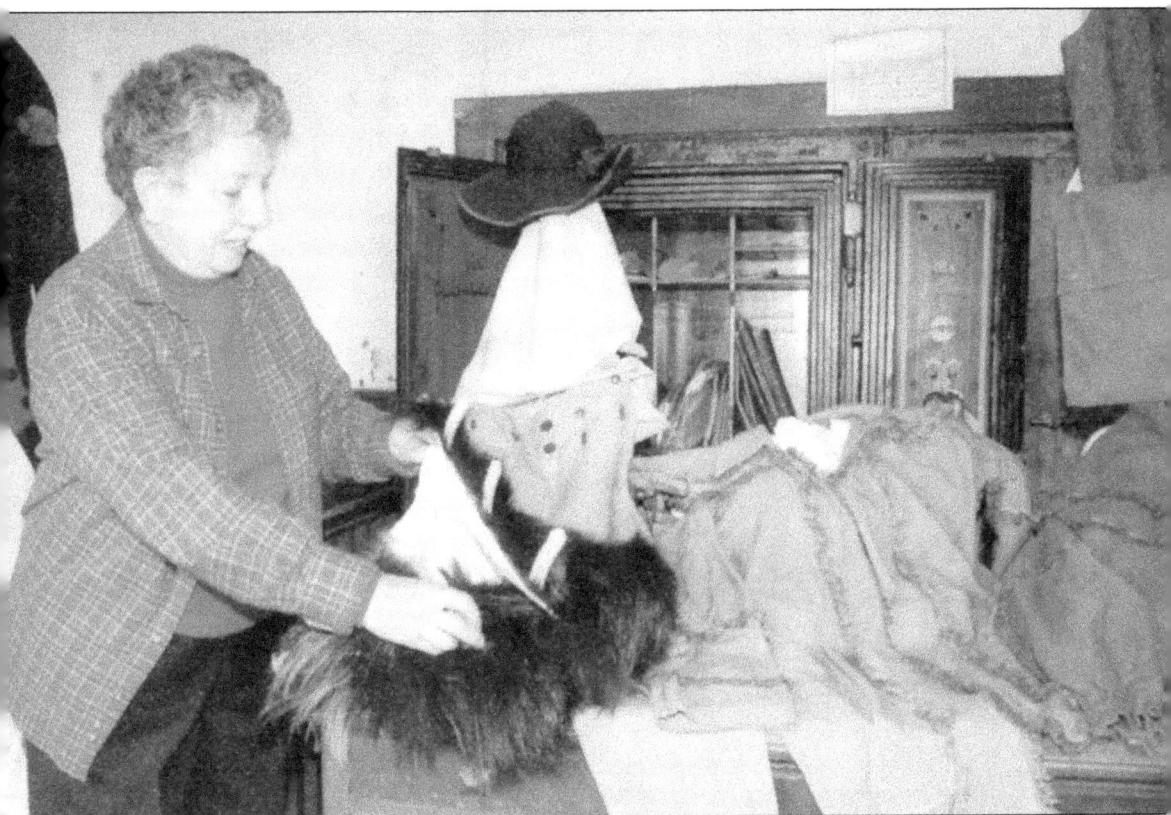

Kathy Barry has been a part of the Textile Heritage Museum at Glencoe since the idea for its formation was born. When the idea for a museum in Glencoe developed, she traveled to some of the old New England towns where the textile industry was born in America to view museums there. At those sites, she developed ideas that could be used in a museum in Glencoe. She worked with Jerrie Nall to develop a trunk museum from which grew the full museum that now occupies the old company store/office building on Front Street in the Glencoe village. Now she helps prepare exhibits for the Glencoe museum, works as a hostess to visitors, and helps in its general operations. Jerrie Nall, Kathy Barry, and other volunteers have spent a tremendous amount of time in sharing the textile story with many visitors to the Textile Heritage Museum over the years. (Courtesy of the *Burlington Times-News*.)

Jerrie Nall (left) and Kathy Barry (right) display a gift made to the museum by the management of Copland Fabrics, Inc., a textile company just downriver from Glencoe, at Hopedale. Copland gave this loom to be displayed in the Textile Heritage Museum, one of a number of gifts made by Alamance County textile companies. Nall and Barry originated the idea for a museum, initially establishing a trunk museum, which operated from 2001 to 2004. When the company store building was purchased, the permanent museum had its beginning. Textile companies in the area have been generous with materials, such as this loom. Displays allow museum visitors to see up close the history of textiles in Alamance County since the early 1800s. In addition to gifts, many individuals have donated their time, restoring the building for this new purpose in a revived Glencoe village.

A coffin might seem to be a strange object in a textile museum, but this one had a place in Glencoe's history. It was used in initiation rites for members inducted into the Order of United American Mechanics, a fraternal organization that had a chapter in Glencoe for many years. There was a lodge hall in the village, and it was surrounded by mystery for those who were not members.

In May 2005, some unique automobiles rolled into Glencoe for a stop at the Textile Heritage Museum. These are Franklin automobiles, classic cars not produced since 1934. These luxury cars were quite popular for many years. However, the company closed its doors in 1934, during the Depression. (Courtesy of the *Burlington Times-News*.)

The Franklin Car Club parked a number of the classic vehicles in front of the museum during the 2005 visit. The Franklin is a favorite of auto collectors, with only about 150,000 made. The museum now attracts a number of visits by special groups each year. Visitors are treated to a tour of the museum and the village. (Courtesy of the *Burlington Times-News*.)

Jerrie Nall, curator of the Textile Heritage Museum, sits at the owner's desk in the Glencoe Mill office, which is now a part of the museum. The portrait on the wall behind her is that of James H. Holt Sr., who took the lead in founding the Glencoe Mill in 1880. (Courtesy of the *Burlington Times-News*.)

Kathy Barry (left), Jerrie Nall (center), and Dr. Sam Powell (right) were the people most involved in the founding of the Textile Heritage Museum. They are on the porch of the museum, which occupies the old company store and mill office building on Front Street in the Glencoe Mill village. (THM.)

This strange machine is a flying shuttle loom, given to the museum by North Carolina State University. It had been used as a teaching loom in the university's school of textiles. This unusual looking item was a vital piece of equipment in textile mills in years past.

World War II had a major impact on the Glencoe Mill village. A number of young men who lived in the village and worked in the mill were called to active duty. Some of them came back home and returned to the mill. Others went into other jobs on their return. Some did not come back, including a member of the family that owned the mill. Holt Green served in the OSS and was captured on a mission behind enemy lines and was executed. Those veterans have been remembered by the Textile Heritage Museum in a number of ways. In 2007, a special Veterans Day program was held in the Glencoe village, sponsored by the museum. A number of veterans from the area, some who once lived in Glencoe, turned out to participate. Here, they are seen on the front steps of the Glencoe Baptist Church on Front Street.

A parade headed by a military honor guard leads the way down Front Street in Glencoe on Veterans Day 2007. The parade moved along the full length of Front Street from Glencoe Baptist Church to the Textile Heritage Museum. Veterans were given special tours of the village during the day.

Vintage automobiles pass in front of the Textile Heritage Museum during the 2007 Veterans Day celebration. A military honor guard was in place on the steps of the museum. Across the street, a military display was set up, including a small encampment area. An exhibit of military weapons was also shown there.

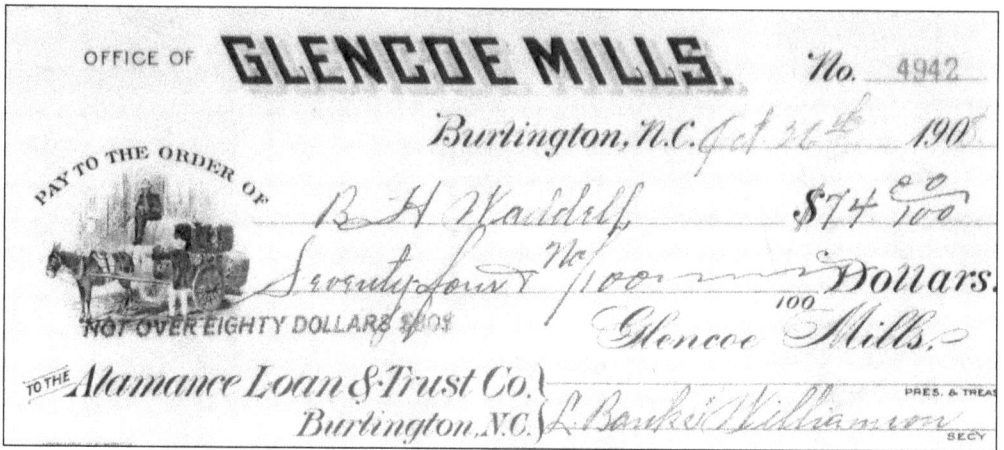

L. Banks Williamson signed this check to B.H. Waddell in 1908 in the amount of $74. There is no indication of what the check might have been for. Glencoe Mill was using Alamance Loan & Trust Co. for its banking at the time. Williamson was corporate secretary in 1908.

In the early days of the nation, few people had access to textile goods produced in a mill. They had to make their own at home, creating what was called a cottage industry. This display shows a loom that might have been used in a home. At the top of the photograph are various spinning wheels, which were found in so many homes in the nation's early history.

The basic raw material of mills in the late 19th and early 20th centuries was cotton. Cotton was grown across much of the South and was shipped to mills for conversion to yarn and, ultimately, cotton fabric. This basket holds cotton as it came from the fields. Cotton ruled until the 1920s, when Burlington Mills began work with rayon, changing the textile history.

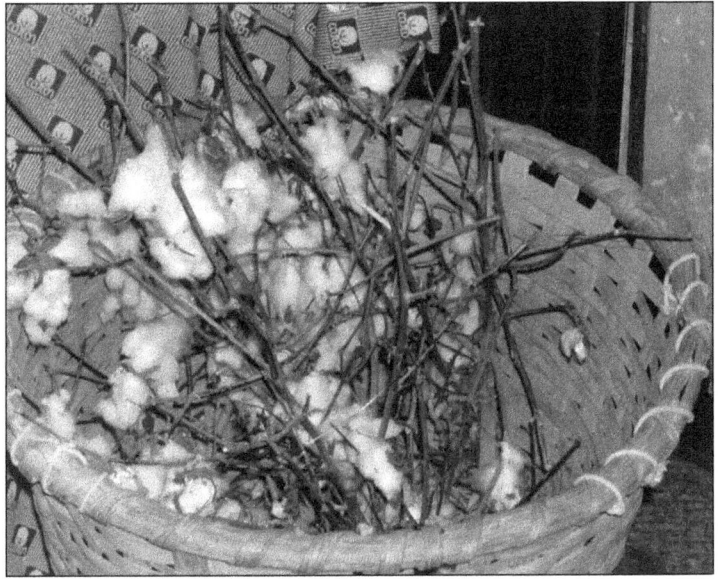

Along one wall of the Textile Heritage Museum is this little model of the Glencoe Mill village as it appeared when the mill opened. The mill is at the far end of the display, with houses along Front and Back Streets. Behind each of the mill houses is a little outhouse building.

James Waddell operated the Glencoe company store for almost 30 years. Those entering this display at the Textile Heritage Museum might believe he is still there. This mannequin looks much as Waddell did in the 1940s. The store display is at the rear of the museum, in the building in which the store was originally located.

This display in the museum shows an array of goods that were sold when the company store occupied the building. Items including groceries, shoes, clothing, and medicines were sold in the store. Village residents did not often have the opportunity to shop outside the village, as there was little transportation available.

When raw cotton was spun into yarn in the mill, it was put on these large spools. They in turn fed the looms that produced the fabric. It was because of cotton that mills appeared in the 19th century up and down Haw River and on Great Alamance Creek. When rayon appeared in the 1920s, a new day dawned in the textile industry.

Compared to the little looms used in homes in the past, this one is a giant. This loom operated at Copland Fabrics at Hopedale for a number of years before it was donated to the museum for display. The loom gives visitors an opportunity to see what actually goes into the production of a fabric they may be wearing or using in their homes.

In the rear of the Textile Heritage Museum is a replica of the company store. Part of the display shows a huge collection of medicines that might have been sold in the store over the years. There are old patent medicines, pain relievers, and tonics that villagers used to keep their health problems in check.

This display, related to the medicine display at the back of the company store area of the museum, shows a number of the more popular medications used in the past. The books include articles describing health care in the years when Glencoe Mill was in operation.

Glencoe Mill had telephone service in the 1890s, thanks to John Q. Gant, who started Glen Raven Mill upriver. He brought the first phone to Burlington to link his mill and his home, and then he connected the service to Glencoe and other mills in the area. The mills shared the cost of equipment and upkeep.

Old typewriters and an adding machine used in Glencoe Mill's office are displayed in front of the company safe. The mill office occupied a part of the building where the Textile Heritage Museum is located. At the rear is the office used by heads of the mill over the years.

Mill families were often large, and money was short, so they used every way possible to meet their needs. For example, feed and flour sacks made of fabric were created into dresses for girls. Feed-sack dresses were widely used, and fabric makers had this in mind when designing patterns to be printed on sacks.

The museum makes a continuing effort to show the various ways in which textile fabrics have been used in the past and today. Displays illustrate various uses, such as this beautiful wedding dress. This dress features some of the most delicate fabrics, produced for their beauty and intended to make the wedding day beautiful and memorable.

Another display shows beautiful curtains, designed to make the home brighter and more cheerful. Copland Fabrics at Hopedale has been a world leader in the production of curtain fabrics for many years. Displays like this are intended to show visitors the many ways in which textile products make homes more comfortable.

Exhibits in the Textile Heritage Museum often focus on an important time in history and show how textiles played a role in it. This display brought World War II to visitors. Other exhibits have featured local history, fashions through the years, quilts, and other things related to Glencoe and its village.

This safe served Glencoe Mill through its years of operation. It is located in the office side of the old company store building. The business office was quite small. There was a little lobby at the front with a glass partition, behind which was the business office. The mill owner's office was at the rear.

These World War II uniforms were part of the military display in the museum a few years ago. Glencoe and other mills converted operations to the production of materials needed for the war effort. J. Spencer Love of Burlington Mills went to Washington to serve as a coordinator for such war production.

North Carolina State University School of Textiles made a display of uniforms, showing the various needs that have to be met by manufacturers. The fireman's uniform has different needs than the ice-hockey uniform or other sports and service-industry uniforms. Textile products have undergone tremendous changes to meet the many demands of specialty users.

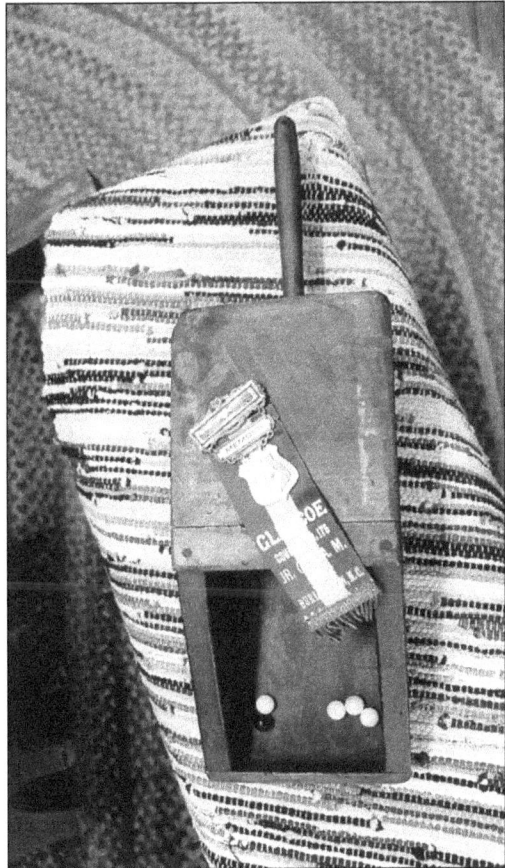

This display shows the voting box for the Order of United American Mechanics, which had a chapter in the village. The fraternal order had its own building. When new members were proposed, this ballot box was used for the vote. White balls were dropped into the box to vote for a candidate, and black balls were used to vote against.

This is a machine from the hosiery industry on display in the museum. Burlington was once home to many major hosiery companies, such as May Hosiery, McEwen Hosiery, Tower Hosiery, Burlington Industries, Glen Raven, and Kayser-Roth. At one time, Burlington had as many as 80 hosiery mills, although some were home operations.

The Textile Heritage Museum focuses on Glencoe Mill, but it recognizes the role of other textile operations in Alamance County. This display shows products made by Burlington Industries. The logo at upper left became known everywhere as the mark of the largest textile manufacturer in the world in the 1960s. The mill began in 1923 in nearby Burlington.

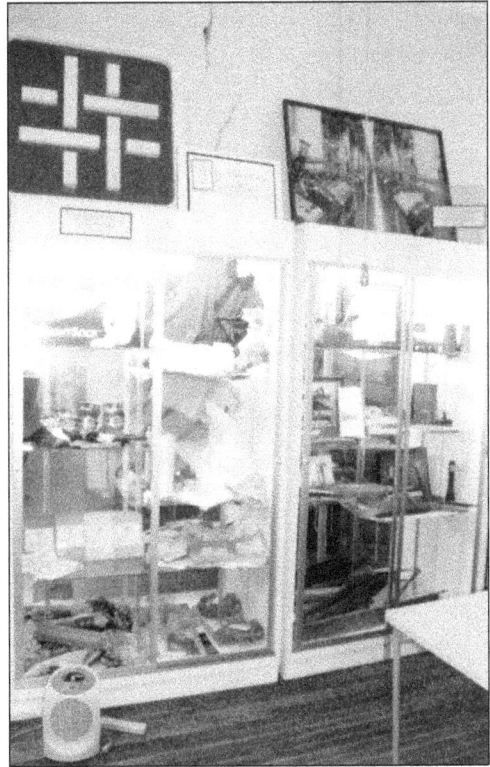

This display features products made at Copland Fabrics, just down Haw River from Glencoe. Copland was formed in 1939 in a location where a mill had existed from the mid-1800s. Copland continues operations today and is a major factor in the economy of Alamance County and a major entity in the nation's textile community.

This card-design machine, donated by Karastan Carpets, was used with looms to produce a desired pattern in carpet. The design is achieved by punching holes in the card to correspond with the intended design on the material being produced. The cloth above the machine shows the pattern produced by the cards in use at the time.

Visitors to the Textile Heritage Museum can learn a lot about cotton. They see it in various forms and in various stages of production in the mill. At this display, they can see and feel cotton in its various stages, including carded cotton, combed and drawn cotton, ginned cotton, and cotton bolls.

This whistle is symbolic of life in the Glencoe Mill village. Life in Glencoe revolved around its piercing scream at various times of the day. It was the village alarm clock as well as the signal that day was done. Alamance County resident Jim Mabry gained possession of the whistle sometime after the mill closed. When the museum opened, he donated it, saying that was the proper place for it. The whistle was used to signal change of shifts at Glencoe Mill. The boiler operator was responsible for blowing the steam whistle. In early years, it was blown for two minutes at 4:30 a.m. to waken workers, and one long blast at 5:45 a.m. gave a 15-minute warning. It was blown for two short blasts at 6:00 a.m. to begin the shift. In later years, the whistle was blown at 6:55 a.m. for work to begin and then again at 3:00 p.m. to signal the second shift to work.

This museum display shows that the proper lady would never leave home without a hat, gloves, and a purse with a "hankie." This, of course, applied to ladies in years past, as few seem to follow that decorum today. All the items on the table are made from various textile products.

This display harkens back to a time when scraps of material would be pieced together and made into a beautiful quilt or throw. Displays change on a continuing basis, and new items are brought in with special textile themes. There is always something new for the many regular visitors.

The Textile Trail marks the location of cotton mills in Alamance County. There were several along Haw River, some on Great Alamance Creek, and others at locations in and around Burlington and Graham. Each of the mills is pictured, with information about operations and directions to those who want to follow the trail.

This is another large loom used in the carpet industry in years past. It is one of four looms donated to the museum by Karastan. The museum has been fortunate to receive such gifts from major textile companies. These gifts help illustrate to visitors the role of textiles in the nation's history.

Spinning wheels of all shapes and sizes are featured in the museum. In the early years of the nation, spinning wheels were part of a home's furnishings, as cotton was spun into yarn and then made into fabric on small looms. Even after textile mills began to fill the nation's needs, many spinning wheels remained in use.

This miniature works just like its larger counterparts, producing material in the same process as the big looms. Looms have come in many sizes over the years, depending on the needs of a particular job. Many of these unique machines are a part of the permanent exhibit at the museum.

Bikers, hikers, and antique automobile clubs like to plan outings where they can travel about the state and enjoy the beauty of the countryside. They also like to sample a bit of the culture along the way, visiting places of historic interest. The Glencoe Mill village provides just such an experience, and many groups take advantage of that opportunity each year now. The Greensboro Car Tour made a stop at the museum in 2008. A number of organizations make such visits over the years as more and more people learn about the museum. School groups take field trips there, and students from Elon University visit often as a part of their work at the school just a few miles from Glencoe. The village is located on NC Highway 62 on the north side of Burlington. It is easily accessed from Interstate 40/85 and US Highway 70.

These uniforms date to World War II. Production of textile mills all across the United States turned to the war effort after the attack on Pearl Harbor in 1941. Fabric was needed not only for uniforms, but for many other purposes as well. The textile industry was a vital factor in supplying military needs during the war.

This tiny loom was another gift to the museum. This miniature of a working loom actually operates, and on it is a piece of the plaid material that made the mills of the E.M. Holt family known throughout the country. It was first produced in the Alamance Mill in 1853.

One of the more memorable exhibits at the Textile Heritage Museum is this one, which features many beautiful quilts. Quilting was another part of the cottage industry of the 1800s, when women made textile products with their own hands and looms. Quilting became an art for many women, as shown in these products.

More quilts and beautiful wall hangings are displayed in the office area of the Glencoe Mill company store building, which now serves as the Textile Heritage Museum. Old pieces and scraps of cloth have been saved and then joined into beautiful patterned quilts. Many skilled seamstresses continue this art today.

The most unusual quilt at the museum features images of the Glencoe Mill and village. Panels show the mill buildings, the houses of the village, and the old churches. It seems appropriate that this quilt gives a good history of a textile village by way of beautiful pictures in fabric.

This is a unique representation of the Glencoe Mill company store and office building. It is one panel of a large quilt that tells the Glencoe story in quilted pictures. The building, the streets, the grassed areas, and surroundings are captured with great accuracy. The quilt is on display in the Textile Heritage Museum, which now occupies this building.

Daily life in the Glencoe Mill village is an important focus for the Textile Heritage Museum. Pictures, items from homes in the village, clothing, and other objects are on display. This is but one exhibit among several illustrating what it was like to live in a mill village between 1880 and 1954.

These two photographs of Pennington family members were found in an old desk in a building in the community. Such photographs are a valuable part of the story told along the walls and aisles of the museum. They show life as it was in another day and add to the story of a mill village and its people.

The part of the company store building that housed the mill office is used for rotating exhibits. This exhibit shows the history of Burlington in photographs. It was broken down into various categories, such as travel, churches, industry, schools, and other elements of the city. Exhibits remain for several weeks and are then replaced.

This is another display offering a pictorial history of Burlington. The panel at left shows the early churches in Burlington. All the denominations represented are still active in Burlington, but they all are in new church facilities. Other areas of the city's history are displayed on the panels extending across the room.

This area of the museum is devoted to the history of the production of textile items in the home. The loom is one that might have served a family in the past. Displays and photographs show the ways in which cotton was turned into clothing, quilts, and other necessities in the home, long before textile mills filled those needs.

This was the cloth that made history in the 1800s. It is the plaid cloth produced in E.M. Holt's mill on Alamance Creek. As his sons and sons-in-law opened new mills, they produced the same product. It was the first commercially dyed cloth to be produced in the South, when textiles were considered a Northern industry.

Visit us at
arcadiapublishing.com

www.ingramcontent.com/pod-product-compliance
Lightning Source LLC
Chambersburg PA
CBHW050626110426
42813CB00007B/1732